Girls'
LACROSSE

by Paul Bowker

GIRLS'

SportsZone

Published by ABDO Publishing Company, PO Box 398166, Minneapolis, MN 55439. Copyright © 2014 by Abdo Consulting Group, Inc. International copyrights reserved in all countries. No part of this book may be reproduced in any form without written permission from the publisher. SportsZone™ is a trademark and logo of ABDO Publishing Company.

Printed in the United States of America,
North Mankato, Minnesota

052013
092013

Editor: Chrös McDougall
Series Designer: Marie Tupy

Photo Credits: Luca DiCecco/Alamy, cover, 1; Maryland Athletics, 5; Gail Burton/AP Images, 6, 10, 33; Cal Sport Media/AP Images, 8, 18, 26, 42; Tom Mihalek/AP Images, 13; M. Spencer Green/AP Images, 15; Michael Dwyer/AP Images, 17; John Strohsacker/LaxPhotos.com, 21, 23, 29, 31, 37; Joel Auerbach/Getty Images Sport/Getty Images, 25; Rich Barnes/Icon SMI, 34, 39; James A. Boardman/Shutterstock Images, 41; Red Line Editorial, 44

Library of Congress Control Number: 2013932517

Cataloging-in-Publication Data

Bowker, Paul.
 Girls' lacrosse / Paul Bowker.
  p. cm. -- (Girls' sportszone)
 ISBN 978-1-61783-988-7 (lib. bdg.)
 Includes bibliographical references and index.
 1. Lacrosse for girls--Juvenile literature.   I. Title.
 796.347--dc23
                                                                2013932517

GIRLS'
SportsZone

Table of Contents

1

Scoring with Jen Adams

I t came with one sweeping move in the 1999 National Collegiate Athletic Association (NCAA) championship game. Jen Adams baffled her opponent. She wowed the coaches. She displayed the type of offensive attack few have ever equaled.

Adams took a pass from University of Maryland teammate Quinn Carney. The ball landed safely in Adams's stick. Then, in one sweeping motion, she backhanded a shot past University of Virginia goalie Liz McCarthy. The goalie never really had a chance to stop it. It was the kind of magical offensive play that can turn a game or win a championship. It was the kind of play that lacrosse attackers wish to copy.

Jen Adams was one of the best scorers in women's college lacrosse history during her time at the University of Maryland.

"Jen was feeling it today," Maryland coach Cindy Timchal said that afternoon, "and I'd have to say she ranks right up there with the top players I've ever coached."

Those words would turn out to be telling. Adams was already an offensive threat almost every time her stick touched the ball. Over her career she became regarded as the best women's lacrosse player not just in the United States, but around the world as well.

Lindsey Munday, *left*, of Northwestern University battles for a loose ball against the University of Virginia in the 2005 national title game.

Adams is a native Australian. At Maryland, she became one of the best college lacrosse players ever. She was named a First Team All-American three times. She was named the US collegiate player of the year three times. And she won—a lot. Maryland won four national titles in Adams's four years on the team. She later became a successful lacrosse coach after graduating in 2001. In 2012 Adams was inducted into the National Lacrosse Hall of Fame.

Adams also had success on the international level. She played in three World Cups for Australia, winning gold once.

Adams's backhand-style goal against Virginia was one moment of athletic genius. She scored four goals and had one assist in the Terrapins' 16–6 victory. The win cinched their fifth consecutive national championship. It also finished off a season in which she scored a school

LINDSEY MUNDAY

Lindsey Munday was a midfielder during her playing days at Northwestern University. She was a strong offensive player for both scoring and passing. Her 128 career assists were a school record when she played. She also scored 140 goals. "She is one of the smartest players I've ever coached," Northwestern coach Kelly Amonte Hiller said. Munday became a dominant player on the world stage, as well. She led the US National Team to the 2009 World Cup championship. Munday had a team-leading 17 goals in seven games. Munday is now the coach at the University of Southern California. Her teachings include quick passing and footwork in the 8-meter (26.2-foot) zone and shooting quickly when coming off the line and toward the goal.

record 71 goals. Adams would later have an 88-goal season. She finished her collegiate career as the best scorer in college history with 267 goals and 445 points.

Adams's success came from a lot of hard work. She also learned a lot from Gary Gait. He is a well-known offensive magician in the men's game. Gait was also an assistant coach at Maryland when Adams played.

"Jen never stops working on anything that will make her stickwork better," Gait said. "While other players are going for a water break, Jen is out on that field working on a new move or a new shot. She truly loves to play the game."

Lindsey Munday, *center*, of Northwestern University battles for a loose ball against the University of Virginia in the 2005 national title game.

Making a Play

In lacrosse, the object is to score. In women's lacrosse, 12 players are on the field for one team. There are restrictions on how many players can be in the offensive zone or defensive zone at the same time. US Lacrosse rules specify no more than seven players may be in the offensive zone. Even considering those complexities, the game comes down to scoring and making a play.

Adams, who coaches at Loyola University Maryland, stresses scoring in her teachings. One of the strategies she teaches for going one-on-one with an opponent is a stutter step. One quick, tricky move, and an attacker can get by the defender.

The offensive skills Adams brought to the game have carried over to today's women's lacrosse. Lindsey Munday scored 140 goals and won two national championships at Northwestern University. Katrina Dowd scored 209 goals at Northwestern. Alyssa Murray, a rising star at Syracuse University, had 74 goals to lead the nation in 2012.

JILL BYERS

The impact of Jill Byers's offensive skills surfaced quickly at the University of Notre Dame. She led the Fighting Irish to their first Final Four in 2006 when she was just a freshman. In 2009, she helped the Irish win their first Big East Conference championship. Byers scored a school-record 262 goals and 336 points during her career. In 2012 she came back to Notre Dame as an assistant coach. After her college career, Byers was on the US Lacrosse National Team for four years.

Kristen Kjellman of Northwestern University shoots and scores against the University of Virginia in the 2005 championship game.

Quick Tip: Shooting Styles

There are four basic shooting styles: overhand, sidearm, backhand, and bounce shots. The overhand shot is the most common and is usually the most effective. To practice this shot, position the head of the stick above your shoulder and even with your ear. When shooting, the best attackers transfer weight from their rear foot to their front foot. A strong wrist movement carries the shot. A sidearm shot provides more speed but less accuracy. A backhand shot, such as the one made by Jen Adams in the 1999 NCAA title game, can surprise the defense. Bounce shots are purposely aimed at the ground. This can cause problems for a goalie because she won't know how the ball will react to the ground.

There are several keys to being a great attacker. One of the most important is having a hard and accurate shot. Shots aimed toward the corners are usually harder for a goalie to save. Speed is also important. So is the ability to show variations in speed. Another key is being able to successfully cradle the ball. Attackers should also be able to avoid stick checks by defenders. A stick check can knock the ball out of an attacker's stick. Location on the field is also important.

"The most dangerous place on a lacrosse field is the island—5 feet (1.52 m) out and 5 feet (1.52 m) up. This is the promised land for every attackman," says Jeff Beeker, a lacrosse coach at Hood College and also an elite coach with Central Maryland club teams.

chapter 2

Passing with Hannah Nielsen

Hannah Nielsen of Northwestern University held the ball behind the University of North Carolina net. She patiently waited for a teammate to be open. She moved from one side of the net to the other side. But she remained behind the goal. As teammate Katrina Dowd cut toward the net, Nielsen passed to her. In less than a second the ball was in the net.

That play showed how accurate a passer Nielsen was in her collegiate career and also with the Australian national team.

Nielsen had five other assists in the game against North Carolina. This helped Northwestern to a 21–7 victory in the 2009 NCAA title game. Her six assists set an NCAA championship-game record. It was a perfect way to

Northwestern's Hannah Nielsen, *left*, and Katrina Dowd, *right*, celebrate Dowd's goal in the 2007 NCAA championship game.

ACACIA WALKER

Acacia Walker became the women's lacrosse coach at Boston College in 2012. She had been a star midfielder long before that. Walker was just 15 years old when she won her first international gold medal with the US Under-19 National Team in 1999. Walker later became an 11-time member of the senior US national team. The highlight was winning a World Cup championship in 2009. Walker also played soccer and basketball in high school. She blossomed into a world-class midfielder while at the University of Maryland. Her 77 career assists ranked among the top 10 in school history through 2012. She believes strong stick skills produce the best players and conducts camps to develop stick skills in players.

finish a collegiate career in which she started every game for the Wildcats. The last game clinched a fifth consecutive national championship for Northwestern. In fact, the Wildcats won all 23 games that year.

"At the beginning of the year, we sort of joked about [being undefeated] and said it was the only thing we hadn't accomplished as a class," Nielsen said.

Nielsen was a big reason for the team's wins. Some consider her the greatest passer in the history of women's lacrosse. It showed in her senior year.

Nielsen led the nation with 142 points in 2009. Her 16 assists in the NCAA tournament set a record. Through 2012, she was the only player to have 10 assists in one game. Her career assists total of 224 is so remarkable that her total broke the previous record by 46 points.

Northwestern University is located just outside Chicago. Nielsen even drew comparisons to another Chicago icon during her time there.

"She has the ability to step up in pressure situations like [former Chicago Bulls basketball star] Michael Jordan, who you always knew would make the big shot," said Kelly Amonte Hiller, Nielsen's coach at Northwestern. "And she has that Larry Bird characteristic of making people around her better."

Amonte Hiller is regarded as one of the world's best coaches. Before coaching she was a great playmaker herself. She averaged more than two assists a game at Maryland and also played for the US National Team.

Hannah Nielsen, *right*, practices with a Northwestern teammate in 2009.

Having the ability to see the entire field and make an accurate pass is a huge skill for a lacrosse player. It is one of Nielsen's strengths. Fellow Australian Jen Adams dominated the game before Nielsen. She noted where Nielsen stands out most.

"Her vision of the field is amazing," Adams said of the Adelaide, Australia, native.

Nielsen has also starred on the international level. She scored 12 goals and had 13 assists in the 2009 World Cup. That helped Australia win a silver medal behind the champion United States. Sue Sofarnos coached Nielsen in both the 2005 and 2009 World Cups.

"She is a magician," Sofarnos said. "She creates time and speed not with her feet, but with her stick and her ability to read the game."

Passing and Catching

The ability to move the ball around the field is important. A defender might pass to a midfielder, and then a midfielder to an attacker or a wing player. Or a goalie might pass to a defender, who will then pass the ball upfield. Passes can also come in fast-break situations. For example, in a two-on-one, an attacker can pass to a teammate when the defender or goalie is expecting a shot. Passes can be 60 yards (54.9 m) across the field or downfield. Passes can also be sent from behind the opponent's net to an attacker, as Nielsen was so good at doing.

Northwestern's Sarah Albrecht, *right*, carries the ball against Duke University during a 2006 playoff game.

Even the most visionary passer will struggle without being fundamentally sound, however. Players such as Nielsen spend hours practicing the basics of passing and catching the ball.

It is most important that a pass be accurate. However, a harder-thrown pass has a better chance of reaching a teammate. If a pass is too slow or is lobbed high in the air, an opposing player will have more time to get in position and possibly intercept it. The most effective pass is an overhand pass. This is when the stick is held up and down at a 45-degree angle to start.

Jacksonville University midfielder Chelsea Watts passes the ball during a 2013 game.

Quick Tip: Practice, Practice, Practice

To practice passing all you need are a few lacrosse balls and a wall to hit them against. By throwing a ball against a wall, you can practice both throwing and catching. The wall should be at least as high as the pass. If there are two players, face each other about 10 yards (9.1 m) apart. Practice overhand passing and receiving. Once that is done well, turn your body so that it is sideways to the wall. Again, practice the throws. As the passing gets better, try moving farther back from the wall while still hitting the same part of the wall with the passes.

Receiving a ball is also important. The receiver should make herself a good target for a pass. This means lining up the face of the pocket to the passer. A receiver should keep the pocket of her stick above her shoulder and keep the stick upright. She should establish space between herself and opposing players. Once the ball lands in the pocket, it is important to immediately cradle the ball so as to keep possession.

Players do not have to be at practice to work on their passing and receiving. Two friends can practice throwing to each other in standing positions and also on the run. In a game, most passing situations will occur while running.

The best offensive players are able to pass *and* shoot. Nielsen scored almost as many goals (59) as she had assists (83) in 2009. That was the year she broke the NCAA single-season record for assists.

chapter **3**

Goalkeeping with Devon Wills

The pressure was high. It was the 2009 World Cup championship game. Former Dartmouth College star Devon Wills was in net for the US National Team. At halftime, the United States and Australia were tied 3–3.

That day in Prague, Czech Republic, turned out to be memorable. Wills had seven saves and three ground balls against the powerful Australians. Her effort helped to lead the United States to an 8–7 victory. Afterward, Wills put on a red, white, and blue American hat. She held the American flag over her head during the team's post-game celebration.

"It's amazing. I've never felt like this," Wills said. "The adrenaline is just pumping. I could play another game right now."

Devon Wills was a star player for both the US National Team and Dartmouth College.

THE BEST, AND BUSIEST, OF ALL TIME

Many goalkeepers have won multiple championships and set records. Morgan Lathrop set a school record at Northwestern with 553 saves. She started 86 games and won 83 times. Sue Heether, who coached the US National Team in 2009, had 312 saves for Loyola Maryland in 1988. That was the second best in NCAA history. But through 2012, only one player in NCAA women's history had reached four figures in career saves. Chris Lindsey, who played at Georgetown University from 1995 to 1998, totaled 1,067 saves. That was 99 more than any other goalie through 2012.

Wills emerged with a gold medal and was named Player of the Match. It was the sixth gold medal for the United States in World Cup play. The World Cup is the biggest tournament in international women's lacrosse. It is held every four years in a different country. The US victory avenged a loss to Australia in the gold-medal game in 2005. Wills called the last 10 seconds of the 2009 title game her best lacrosse moment.

Wills made the US National Team after finishing a four-year career at Dartmouth. While there, she was named an All-American three times. In her freshman year of 2003, Wills was named the Ivy League Rookie of the Year. Her 538 saves were second in school history. She started every game except one.

Wills had a goals-against average of 6.69 in the 2009 World Cup. US coach Sue Heether said: "We are the best in the world at keeping that cage protected."

In the World Cup championship game, Australia scored seven goals. However, Wills gave up just five goals. At one point in the game she pushed Australian attacker Marlee Paton. The officials gave Wills a yellow card. That resulted in a three-minute penalty. Wills had to leave the field. The team was able to use a backup goalie but had to play short a player during the penalty. The Australians scored two goals during her absence. Wills returned to the game with less than two minutes left. She promptly made a save that preserved the one-goal victory.

The series showed the importance of a strong goalkeeper and how much a penalty can hurt a team.

Devon Wills gets ready to pass the ball to a Team USA teammate.

MIKEY MEAGHER

Great goalkeeping performances can win games. Mikey Meagher showed off her goalie skills in a 2012 game. Meagher's University of Florida squad beat top-ranked Northwestern 14–7 in the American Lacrosse Conference tournament finals. Meagher was named tournament Most Valuable Player. However, she credited the play of her team's overall defense for her success. Meagher led the nation in both save percentage (.537) and goals-against average (7.03) in 2012. She became the third goalie to do so since the NCAA began recording those statistics in 1996.

The Final Line of Defense

In a traditional lacrosse game, seven field players are allowed in the defensive zone. The goalkeeper is the last line of defense behind them. Lacrosse is such a fast-moving game that shutouts are rare. However, a good goalkeeper can make a huge difference, especially in close games. The goalkeeper needs to stop as many shots as possible and then clear the ball to a teammate to start a counterattack.

Only the goalkeeper, or her deputy, may occupy the space of the 8.5-foot (2.6-m) goal circle. Any other defender or attacker who crosses the line is subject to a goal-circle foul. That isolation makes a goalie's technique and positioning especially important because no defenders can block a close-range shot. Goalkeepers should keep the head of their sticks upright and maintain a strong stance. Better positioning gives the attacker less open space at which to aim. Goalies should shift their bodies to stay in line with the attacker.

A goalkeeper also has different equipment than field players. One big difference is the stick. A goalkeeper's stick has a bigger pocket than that of field players. The larger stick helps to stop or block shots. Plastic sticks are ideal because they are lighter than wood sticks and easier to control.

University of Florida goalie Mikey Meagher, *right*, stops a shot by Syracuse University in 2013.

Goalkeepers also have more protective equipment than field players. This includes a helmet, a chest protector, a throat protector, goalie gloves, and leg padding.

A goalkeeper's primary job is to prevent goals from being scored. It is also important for the goalkeeper to maintain a strong mental balance. No lacrosse goalkeeper can stop every shot. The key for the goalie is to always be ready for the next challenge, no matter what happened before. A goalie cannot get rattled, Northwestern coach Kelly Amonte Hiller wrote in her

Delaware goalie Alex Zaugra saves a shot by Loyola Maryland during a 2012 game.

Quick Tip: Making Saves

Fundamentals are key. Remember to keep your stick flat to the shooter. Keep your hands and elbows in front of your body. Positioning is important, too. If an attacker goes behind the net with the ball, the goalie should remain in front of the net with her stick up. She should be ready to move quickly to the post when the attacker comes around to that side. To practice, get a couple of teammates. Have them stand several yards away in a semicircle facing the net. Then have each player take turns shooting. This will help you get a feel for positioning and where to stand for shots that come from different angles.

book. A goalie must reset quickly after a goal is scored. Former Loyola Maryland goalkeeper Trish Dabrowski agrees.

"If a team scores on you two or three times in a row, it's easy to falter," Dabrowski said. "A great goalie can bounce back from that and learn to separate their mistakes from the mistakes of their teammates. Remember, the ball's got to get through eleven other players to get to you."

Amonte Hiller said a great way for goalkeepers to practice is to face tennis balls from close range. A coach or teammate propels tennis balls toward the cage from just a few yards away with an attacker's stick. The goalkeeper must attempt to step up and knock the ball away with the shaft of her stick, not the pocket. Using tennis balls helps develop quick hand-eye coordination.

chapter 4

Defending with Gina Oliver

G ina Oliver's passion for playing strong defense goes back to her high school days in Pottstown, Pennsylvania. She later became an All-World defender and two-time member of the US National Team.

"She was a field general," her high school coach Andy Bachman said. "She was the one calling plays, directing traffic, telling people where to go and what to do. She was one of the reasons why—not just for the years she was here, but after she left—we had such a strong team."

At Pottstown High School, Oliver was a star and team leader even as a sophomore. Her strong play led to a record-setting playing career at Ohio State University. Ohio State was not known as a powerhouse program.

Gina Oliver, *left*, was a top defensive player for Ohio State University and Team USA.

THE BEST AT TURNOVERS

Moira Muthig's breakout year in 2000 has never been equaled. Muthig was a defender at Manhattan College. That year she had an NCAA record of 82 caused turnovers in just 14 games. That is an average of nearly six caused turnovers per game. But over a four-year college career, Georgetown University's Michi Ellers was the first to top 200 caused turnovers. She finished with a record 204. She went on to play with the US National Team and coach at Georgetown. Ellers said that "hard work and determination" is what leads to success.

Oliver helped the Buckeyes claim one of their biggest wins ever, though. As a sophomore in 2002, Oliver led her team to a 12–11 win over Maryland. The Terrapins were seven-time defending champions at the time.

Later she helped the US National Team win a gold medal at the 2009 World Cup. Oliver played a key defensive role in the championship game against Australia. The game was close and had a dramatic finish. That made every goal that much more important. Ultimately, Oliver's tight defense helped the United States claim an 8–7 victory.

Through her playing years, and later as a coach, Oliver has always displayed her passion for defense. She is an attacking defender.

"You've got to have a little bit of an attitude when you're playing defense. You can't just go out on the field and do what you want,"

Oliver said. "I don't like to sit back and see what the offense does. I'm very proactive."

Oliver was an All-American three times at Ohio State. She set school records for caused turnovers (201) and ground balls (236). She went into college coaching after her collegiate playing career ended. Not surprisingly, she became a defensive specialist. Oliver was defensive coordinator for five years at Duquesne University in Pittsburgh. Then she became head coach at the University of Cincinnati. Oliver is an example of what a great defensive player can become.

Team USA player Gina Oliver, *left*, guards an opponent.

CHRISTY FINCH

Christy Finch was one of the top defenders in NCAA history. She helped lead Northwestern to national championships in all four of her years with the Wildcats. Her 70 caused turnovers in 2008 led the nation. She totaled 183 caused turnovers in her collegiate career. That ranked fourth all-time in the NCAA through 2012. In addition, she was the 2008 national defender of the year and a two-time All-American. Following her playing career, Finch went on to become an assistant coach at Ohio State University. There, she specialized in defense.

"It hasn't set in yet," Oliver said while visiting her hometown shortly after winning a gold medal at the 2009 World Cup. "But every day I wake up, I'm a world champion. Every day people call and people congratulate me, it feels surreal."

Causing Turnovers

Oliver says a defender cannot wait for the play to come to her. A defender must take on an attacker through speed and positioning. It is not until high school that stick checking is allowed. Playing the body is legal in the men's game. However, it is not legal in women's lacrosse. Too much physical play will draw a whistle from the referee.

Causing turnovers and intercepting passes or picking up ground balls is the job of every defender. And once a defender has the ball, she must cradle the ball and pass it up to a midfielder or attacker on her team.

Defenders must communicate with each other and with the goalkeeper constantly. Sometimes defenders might yell "switch" in order to switch the attackers they are guarding. This can prevent other teams from finding open areas to attack. Defenders also must prevent breakaways on the goalkeeper and know when to take on the shooter in a two-on-one break. These instincts come from a lot of practice and guidance from coaches.

Northwestern's Christy Finch, *left*, battles with a Dartmouth College player during a 2005 NCAA playoff game.

33

Northwestern coach and former US National Team star Kelly Amonte Hiller said the sliding concept is key in defending properly. Sliding is the technical name for backing up a teammate. If one defender gets beat, the sliding concept ensures another defender slides over to help out. Coaches introduce this concept as players get more advanced.

Seven defenders, plus the goalkeeper, are allowed on the defensive side of the field. They will guard no more than seven attackers. No more than seven players from one team can be on the offensive side of the field.

Northwestern's Kerri Harrington, *right*, gets into position to defend a Maryland attacker during the 2011 NCAA championship game.

Quick Tip: Picking a Side

The key for a defender is keeping herself between the attacker and the net at all times, and then recognizing which direction the attacker actually wants to go. Watch the attacker's eyes. This can provide a big hint as to where the attacker wishes to go. Also notice which hand is at the top of her stick. If an attacker has her right hand at the top, then she is likely to go toward her right and shoot that way. A lefty is more likely to go left. A good drill to practice takes just one teammate. The attacker has the ball and sets up with her back to the net. The defender stands a few yards in front. When the play begins, the attacker will attempt to go right or left, and then shoot. The defender should practice staying in front of that attacker, moving side to side. The plan is to force a bad shot and maybe even a turnover. Practice this against both left-handers and right-handers.

Defenders may use longer sticks than other players. But before adopting a longer stick, a player should make sure it is a good fit. If a player chokes up too much on a longer stick, then she is better off with a shorter stick. After all, confidence plays a big part in being a strong defender. And the best way to gain confidence is to practice and get more positive experience.

chapter 5

Draw Control with Alyssa Leonard

T he NCAA women's lacrosse championship was on the line in May 2012. Northwestern's Alyssa Leonard was not going to be denied. She towered over Syracuse University's Kailah Kempney on a draw in the center circle. She won possession on the draw to give her Wildcats an immediate advantage. Then they went on to win the game 8–6. It was Northwestern's seventh national championship in eight years.

Leonard was just a sophomore at the time. Still she won six draw controls. Her 90 draw controls in 2012 were the third-highest total in Northwestern history. It was just one behind the 91 she had as a freshman in 2011. The Northwestern record is 110, posted by Danielle Spencer in 2010.

Northwestern's Alyssa Leonard, *right*, is a standout on draws.

KRISTEN KJELLMAN

Three-time All-American and five-time US National Team star midfielder Kristen Kjellman credits her strong stick skills for her success. Kjellman won three straight NCAA titles with Northwestern. She was the first lacrosse player, man or woman, to win the Tewaaraton Trophy in consecutive seasons. The Tewaaraton is annually given to the best women's and men's college lacrosse player.

Kjellman finished her Northwestern career as the NCAA all-time leader in draw controls with 268. Kjellman continued that domination in the center circle for the national team. She had a team-best 20 draw controls at the 2009 World Cup. She retired from international play in 2011. Kjellman also scored a school-record 250 goals for Northwestern.

Draw controls have been a big part of Northwestern's lacrosse program since coach Kelly Amonte Hiller arrived in 2001. Possession, she says, is the most defining factor in a game.

Through 2012, Northwestern teams had recorded three of the top five single-season draw control totals in NCAA history. Northwestern players also had three of the top 15 single-season draw control totals in NCAA history. The school's dominance on draw controls showed in the 2012 NCAA tournament. The Wildcats won 25 of 34 draws in the semifinals and finals. Among those draw controls were eight straight in the championship game.

A Northwestern loss to Florida in 2012 drove home the importance of draws. The Gators defeated Northwestern at their own game. Florida won 18 of 23 draws. That never happened again in 2012.

"I feel we have a tradition of very strong draws," Amonte Hiller said. "I felt I was failing the team not giving the kids enough coaching. I think Alyssa really took it to heart. She was on a mission to get better and to do better. She's so talented. Since that [Florida] game she's been unbelievable."

Leonard, a 5-foot-8 (1.73 m) midfielder, has enjoyed dominant days with Northwestern. She had 10 draw controls in a 2011 game versus

Northwestern midfielder Alyssa Leonard (2) battles with Maryland's Brandi Jones (4) for a loose ball in the 2011 championship game.

AN EYE ON THE GROUND

Snagging ground balls is an effective way to grab possession for a scoring chance. Few teams have been better at it than the University of Delaware teams in the 1980s. Four of the top five ground ball statistical leaders in NCAA history all played at Delaware between 1983 and 1989. Leading that list is Anne Wilkinson. She totaled 466 ground balls from 1983 to 1986. The Blue Hens won a national title her freshman year. Her talent for scooping ground balls clearly came from her experience in field hockey. Wilkinson was a two-time All-American in field hockey at Delaware while also playing lacrosse. She is now the coach of the Ohio State field hockey team.

the Naval Academy. She had nine in a 2012 game against Stanford University. But the 2012 title game against Syracuse stands out.

"I was really looking to get the ball straight up and hopefully beat my girl as far as quickness and getting my hands to the ball first, and it worked for me today," Leonard said.

Beginning with the 2013 season, Leonard was learning from the best. Spencer returned to Northwestern as an assistant coach after the 2012 season. She had been a two-time All-American. Spencer's 203 draw controls ranked second in Northwestern history and twelfth in NCAA history through 2012. At 6-foot-2 (1.88 m), Spencer was an intimidator in center circle.

Center Circle Draw

Draws are important for one simple reason: they determine possession of the ball. The lacrosse draw is similar to an opening tip-off in basketball or a face-off in ice hockey. If a team gets the ball, it can try to score. Winning draws is a good way to ensure that a team gets more possessions and more chances to score.

"If you don't win the draw, you can't have more opportunities on the offense," says Gary Gait, the Syracuse women's lacrosse coach who won three men's national titles with Syracuse as a player.

There are several draws in each lacrosse game. There is always a draw to start the game and at the beginning of the second half. In addition, there

A referee sets up a draw during a 2009 high school game in Oregon.

is a draw after each goal. So in a 15–14 game, for example, there would be 31 draws.

In a draw, two players, one from each team, line up facing each other inside the center circle. Four players from each team stand around the edge of the circle. The two players in the middle hold their sticks horizontally at waist-high level with the pockets facing in. The referee then places the ball between the two sticks in the back of each basket. The two sticks push together to hold the ball. When the whistle sounds, the players immediately try to get their stick under the ball to fling it up

Virginia's Lauren Goerz, *left*, and Syracuse's Kailah Kempney, *right*, battle for a center circle draw during a 2013 game.

Quick Tip: Cradling

Cradling the ball in the pocket of the stick is the way a player maintains possession. Northwestern coach Kelly Amonte Hiller compares cradling in lacrosse to dribbling in basketball or stick handling in ice hockey. She says a player should maintain a triple-threat position when cradling, always face the target, and never stand still. A stationary player who is cradling creates a vulnerability to a defender. Amonte Hiller says players should keep their arms away from the body while cradling and protect their stick from defenders.

and to a teammate. Leaping ability and quick stick skills are important to winning draws.

Draws in women's lacrosse differ from those in the men's game. In men's lacrosse, the ball is placed on the ground between the sticks of two squatting players. The face-off begins with the whistle.

The player in the center circle can only do so much on a draw. The players around the edge of the circle have to do their part too. Amonte Hiller teaches her players to spread out to different areas of the field during a draw. This allows a team to cover more space. That in turn increases the chances of her team possessing the ball. Amonte Hiller said deception can be used to fool an opponent. She tells her players to start out in a different space from where they will end up.

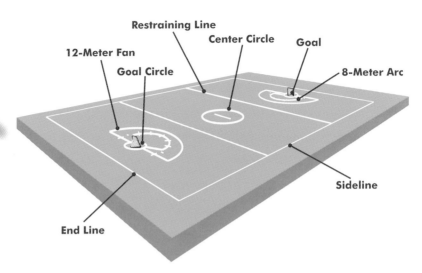

Restraining Line
Center Circle
Goal
12-Meter Fan
8-Meter Arc
Goal Circle
Sideline
End Line

arc and fan

The women's field includes marking for an 8-meter (26.2-foot) arc and a 12-meter (39.4-foot) fan. The arc and fan are used to determine fouls and positioning after major fouls are whistled.

center circle

This is where the draws are held to begin a half or restart play after a goal. The center circle has a radius of 30 feet (9.1 m).

end lines and sidelines

These lines form the boundary of a lacrosse field.

goal circle

This is a circle with a radius of 8.5 feet (2.6 m). Only the goalkeeper, or her deputy, may be inside the goal circle.

restraining line

This is the line that separates one group of players from another. Only seven defenders plus a goalkeeper and seven attackers may be inside the restraining line on either side of the field.

assist

A pass that leads directly to a goal.

attacker

It is an attacker's job to score goals. There are three attackers in the offensive zone.

cradle

To hold the ball in the pocket of a lacrosse stick while running.

draw controls

The face-off between two opposing players inside the center circle. Controlling the draw leads to possession of the ball.

ground ball

When the ball falls from the stick pocket to the ground.

midfielder

A player who is between the offense and defense, often situated toward the middle of the field.

stutter step

A step used to confuse an opponent. A player will go in one direction, change speed with her feet, and then go in another direction.

turnover

When one team loses possession of the ball to the other team.

wing player

A player on the outside left or outside right portions of the field.

Selected Bibliography

American Sport Education Program. *Coaching Youth Lacrosse.* Champaign, IL: Human Kinetics, 1997.

Amonte Hiller, Kelly. *Winning Women's Lacrosse.* Champaign, IL: Human Kinetics, 2010.

Bach, Greg; National Alliance for Youth Sports. *Coaching Lacrosse for Dummies.* Indianapolis, IN: Wiley Publishing, 2008.

Hinkson, Jim. *Lacrosse Fundamentals.* New York: Triumph Books, 2012.

Roberts, M. B. *Lacrosse: The Player's Handbook.* New York: Sterling Publishing, 2007.

Further Readings

Tometich, Annabelle. *Lacrosse.* Minneapolis, MN: ABDO Publishing Co., 2012.

Urick, David. *Sports Illustrated Lacrosse: Fundamentals for Winning.* Lanham, MD: Taylor Trade Publishing, 2008.

Vennum, Thomas, Jr. *American Indian Lacrosse.* Washington, DC: Smithsonian Institution, 1994.

Web Links

To learn more about lacrosse, visit ABDO Publishing Company online at **www.abdopublishing.com**. Web sites about lacrosse are featured on our Book Links page. These links are routinely monitored and updated to provide the most current information available.

Places to Visit

Reverend Harold Ridley, S.J., Athletic Complex

2221 West Cold Spring Lane
Baltimore, MD 21211
(410) 617-1420
www.loyolagreyhounds.com/facilities/locl-ridley.html

Ridley Athletic Complex, which is located on the Loyola Maryland campus in lacrosse-crazed Baltimore, is one of the premier college lacrosse stadiums in the country. It was built in 2010 to house the university's lacrosse and soccer teams.

The US Lacrosse Museum & National Hall of Fame

113 W. University Parkway
Baltimore, MD 21210
(410) 235-6882, ext. 122
www.uslacrosse.org/museum/halloffame.phtml

This museum and hall of fame honors the history of lacrosse along with its greatest players and contributors. Artifacts, memorabilia, and art spanning from the Native American origins of lacrosse through today are featured. The Hall of Fame Gallery has interactive information about the hall of famers who have had the greatest impact on the sport. The museum also features a multimedia show and a documentary about lacrosse.

ABOUT THE AUTHOR

Paul D. Bowker is a freelance writer and author based in Chesterton, Indiana. His 25-year newspaper career includes several years as a lacrosse writer in Massachusetts. He is national past president of Associated Press Sports Editors and has won several national and state writing awards. He lives with his wife and daughter.